My first
100
WORDS

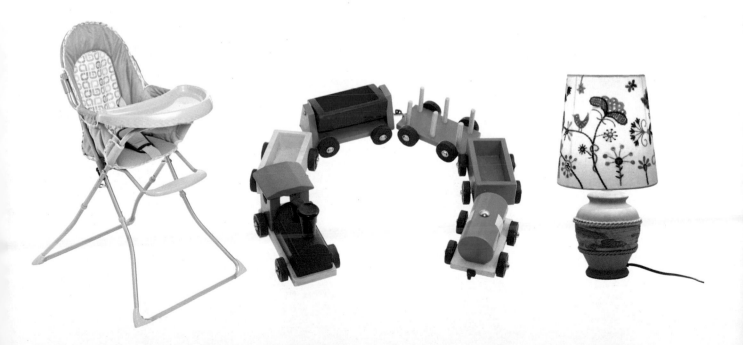

fruits

mango

watermelon

apple

pineapple

cherry

pomegranate

guava

banana

vegetables

cauliflower

pumpkin

carrot

zucchini

radish

cabbage

green pea

food

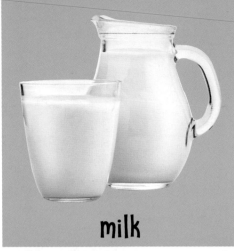
milk

rice

sandwich

egg

cereal

soup

cheese

ice cream

pets & farm animals

dog

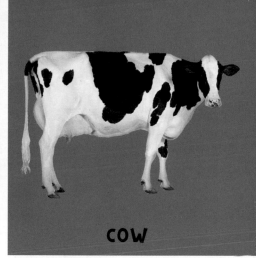

cow

sheep

cat

horse

goat

camel

donkey

wild animals

tiger

lion

elephant

giraffe

zebra

deer

fox

wolf

birds

peacock

owl

duck

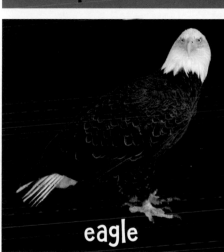
eagle

pigeon

woodpecker

kingfisher

baby objects

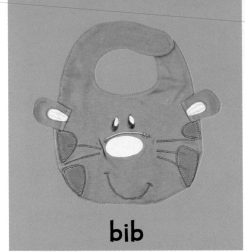

bib

bowl

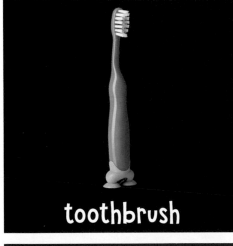

toothbrush

high
chair

bathtub

romper

crib

baby pillow

milk bottle

overalls

baby rocker

stroller

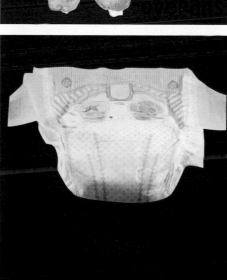

sipper

baby toys

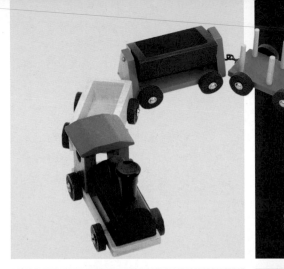

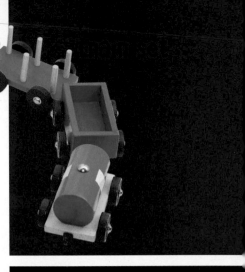

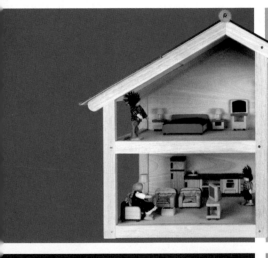

dollhouse

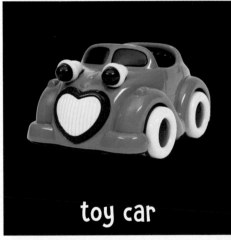

toy car

rocking horse

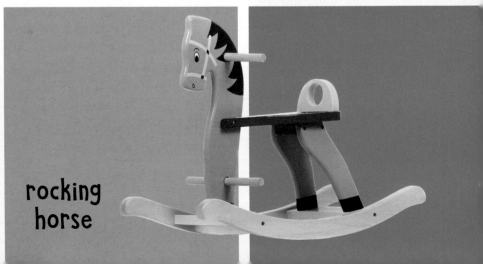

ball

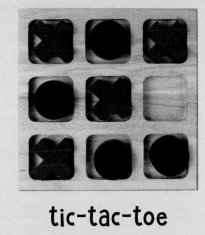

tic-tac-toe

soft toy

frisbee

blocks

doll

abacus

rattle

things at home

sofa

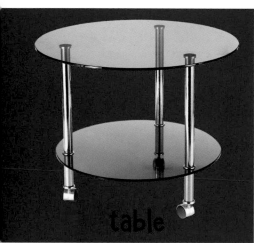
table

television

wardrobe

bed

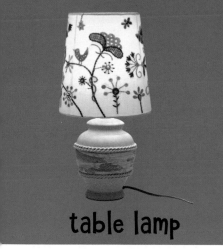

table lamp

refrigerator

carpet

clock

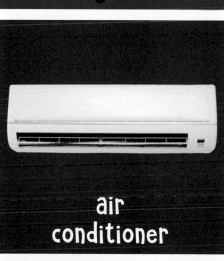

air
conditioner

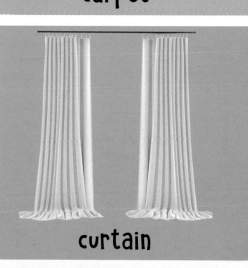

curtain

doormat

telephone

key

things that go

airplane

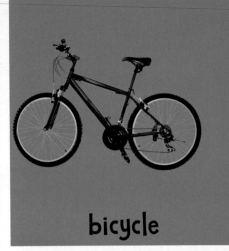

bicycle

motorcycle

car

train

ship

boat

colors

red

tomato

yellow

sunflower

orange

basketball

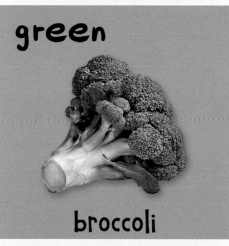

green

broccoli

blue

butterfly

pink

flamingo

black

crow

white

polar bear

my body parts

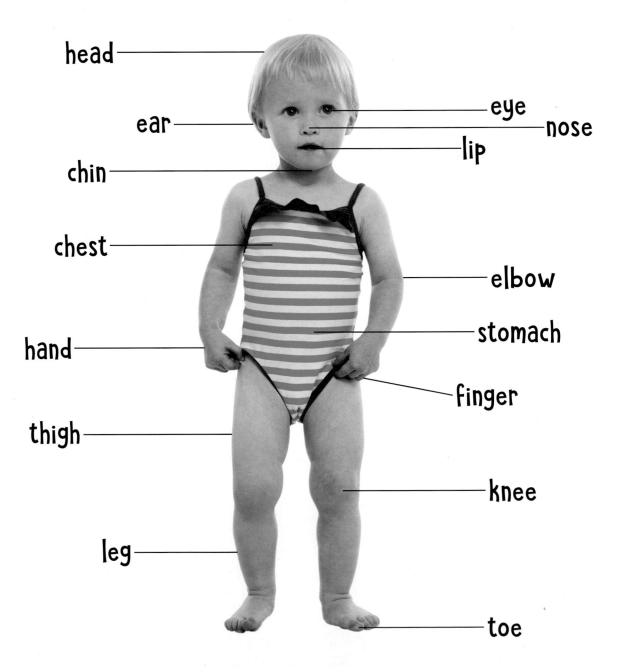

head

ear

chin

chest

hand

thigh

leg

eye

nose

lip

elbow

stomach

finger

knee

toe